SHOTGUN SHOOTING

BOY SCOUTS OF AMERICA
IRVING, TEXAS

Requirements

1. Do the following:

   a. Explain why BB and pellet air guns must always be treated with the same respect as firearms.

   b. Describe how you would react if a friend visiting your home asked to see your or your family's firearm(s).

   c. Explain the need, use, and types of eye and ear protection.

   d. Explain the main points of the laws for owning and using guns in your community and state.

   e. Explain how hunting is related to the wise use of renewable wildlife resources.

   f. Explain the main points of hunting laws in your state and give any special laws on the use of guns or ammunition.

   g. List the kinds of wildlife that can be legally hunted in your state.

   h. Identify and explain the shotgun sports shot in the Olympic Games. Identify places in your community where you could shoot these sports.

   i. List the sources that you could contact for information on firearms and their use.

2. Do ONE of the following options:

   **Option A—Shotgun Shooting
   (Modern Cartridge Type)**

   a. Identify the principal parts of a shotgun, action types, and how they function.

   b. Identify the rules for safe gun handling.

33331
ISBN 0-8395-3331-4
©1989 Boy Scouts of America
2000 Printing of the 1989 Edition

c. Demonstrate how to handle shotguns in a safe manner.

d. Identify the parts of a shotgun shell and their functions.

e. Identify the various gauges of shotguns. Explain which one you would pick for use and why.

f. Identify and demonstrate the five fundamentals of shooting a shotgun.

g. Identify and explain each rule for shooting a shotgun safely.

h. Demonstrate the knowledge, skill, and attitude necessary to safely shoot moving targets, using the fundamentals of shotgun shooting.

i. Identify the materials needed to clean a shotgun.

j. Demonstrate how to clean a shotgun safely.

k. Discuss what points you would consider in selecting a shotgun.

l. Shooting score required—Hit at least 24 (48 percent) out of 50 targets (two 25-target rounds). The two rounds do not need to be shot in consecutive order.

Shooting skill rules:

- Targets may be thrown by a hand trap, manual mechanical, or on any trap or skeet field. Note: If using a hand trap or manual mechanical trap, the trap operator should be at least 5 feet to the right and 3 feet to the rear of the shooter. If throwing left-handed with a hand trap, this should be reversed.

- All targets should be thrown at a reasonable speed and in the same direction.

- Targets should be generally thrown so as to climb in the air after leaving the trap.

- Scores may be fired at any time, either in formal competition or in practice.

- Any gauge shotgun not exceeding 12 gauge may be used.

- Any ammunition, either factory or hand loaded, may be used.

- Shooters must shoot in rounds of 25. Rounds need not be shot continuously or on the same day (the term "round" refers to a single series of 25 shots).

Option B—Muzzle-Loading Shotgun Shooting

a. Discuss a brief history of the development of the muzzle-loading shotgun.

b. Identify principal parts of percussion and flintlock shotguns and discuss how they function.

c. Demonstrate and discuss safe handling rules of a muzzle-loading shotgun.

d. Identify the various grades of black powder and their proper use.

e. Discuss proper safety procedures pertaining to black powder use and storage.

f. Discuss proper components of a load.

g. Identify proper procedures and accessories used for loading a muzzle-loading shotgun.

h. Demonstrate the knowledge, skill, and attitude necessary to safely shoot a muzzle-loading shotgun on a range, including range procedures.

i. Shoot a moving target with a muzzle-loading shotgun using the five fundamentals of firing the shot.

j. Identify the materials needed to clean a muzzle-loading shotgun safely.

k. Demonstrate how to clean a muzzle-loading shotgun safely.

l. Identify the causes of a muzzle-loading shotgun's failing to fire and explain or demonstrate proper correction procedures.

m. Discuss what points you would consider if selecting a muzzle-loading shotgun.

n. Shooting score required—Hit at least 5 out of 15 targets. Shooting skill rules:

- Targets may be thrown by a hand trap, manual mechanical, or on any trap or skeet field. Note: If using a hand trap or manual mechanical trap, the trap operator should be at least 5 feet to the right and 3 feet to the rear of the shooter. If throwing left-handed with a hand trap, this should be reversed.

- All targets should be thrown at a reasonable speed and in the same direction.

- Targets should be generally thrown so as to climb in the air after leaving the trap.

- Scores may be fired at any time, either in formal competition or in practice.

- Any gauge shotgun not exceeding 10 gauge may be used.

- Standard clay targets customarily used for trap and skeet are to be used.

Contents

Shotgun Parts

Your shotgun is a precision instrument. It's designed to shoot a shot charge in a specific pattern that will cover a designed area at a certain distance. Unlike a rifle, the bore of the shotgun is not rifled, so the shot emerging from the muzzle is not spinning.

Your shotgun is built to last a lifetime. By itself, the shotgun poses no greater threat to person or property than any other machine. If you understand your gun—how it works and how to care for it—shooting will be pleasurable and rewarding.

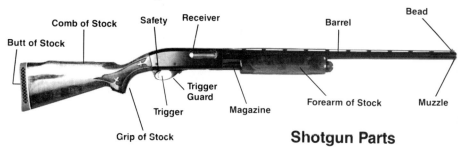

Comb of Stock   Safety   Receiver   Barrel   Bead

Butt of Stock

Trigger Guard

Trigger   Magazine   Forearm of Stock   Muzzle

Grip of Stock

Shotgun Parts

The Stock

The stock is the gun's handle. It has a special significance in proper shooting. It is designed to let you point and shoot accurately. Each part of the stock has a special name.

The butt is the rear end of the stock. It's the part that rests against your shoulder when you point the shotgun.

The comb is the part of the stock that is brought to your cheek as you assume the shooting position.

The grip is the part of the stock held with the trigger hand. It is sometimes referred to as "the small of the stock" because it is where the stock narrows.

The part of the stock that lies under the barrel is called the forearm. On most shotguns, the forearm is separate from the rest of the stock.

The Barrel

The barrel is the metal tube through which the shot passes on its way to the target. The inside portion of the barrel is called the bore. The diameter of the bore will vary depending on the size and use of the gun. Most shotgun bores are designated by a term known as *gauge*. The smaller the gauge number, the larger the bore size.

Starting with the largest bore, modern shotguns are available in 10, 12, 20, and 28 gauge. The lone exception to this measuring system is the .410 bore shotgun. This is often mistakenly referred to as the .410 gauge. It is actually a 67 gauge. This, the smallest of the modern shotguns, has a bore measured by the same standards as rifles and pistols. The .410 shotgun has a bore that is 410/1,000 of an inch in diameter.

Popular Shotshell Gauges

Modern shotguns are loaded at the rear (or breech) end of the barrel by inserting a round of ammunition known as the shotshell. That portion of the barrel into which the shotshell is placed is known as the chamber. The front of the barrel—through which the shot exits the gun—is called the muzzle.

Most shotguns have, near the muzzle, a constriction called the choke. The choke is important. Because shot begins to spread out on exiting the muzzle, the more constricted the shot is at the time it's expelled, the farther it will travel as a compact group. This constriction is determined by the extent of the choke. The greater the choke, the greater the constriction and generally the greater the effective range of the gun and shot pattern.

Chokes and Their Function

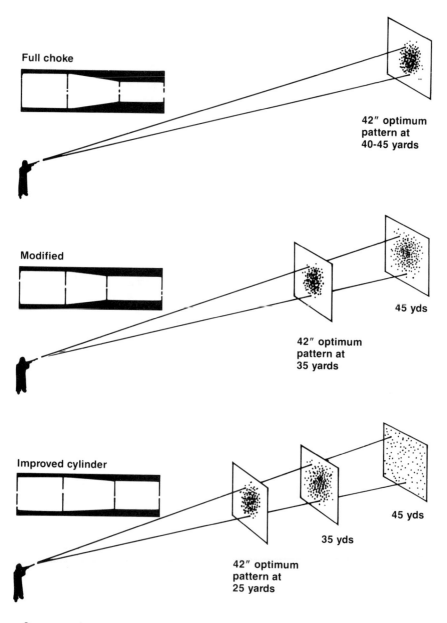

Full choke

42″ optimum
pattern at
40-45 yards

Modified

45 yds

42″ optimum
pattern at
35 yards

Improved cylinder

45 yds

35 yds

42″ optimum
pattern at
25 yards

Most commonly, a full-choke shotgun barrel has the most constriction and the greatest range. However, at close range a full-choke pattern may be too small to consistently hit moving targets or so dense that game is ruined by blanket shot.

Modified choke creates somewhat less constriction. Improved cylinder choke provides for even less constriction. This will provide a shot pattern that widens out quicker than the preceding two. A shotgun barrel that has no choke at all is referred to as cylinder bore. Generally, choke designations are indicated on the outside of the barrel.

Many companies today manufacture shotguns with interchangeable screw-in chokes. Or, a single device known as an adjustable choke can be placed on the end of the barrel. This device allows different choke selections to be made simply by adjusting it to the desired setting. Both of these options are good if only one gun is wanted.

The sighting mechanism on shotguns is rather simple. One or sometimes two beads are positioned on the top of the barrel to help the shooter point at the target. Some shotguns have a rib instead of the beads. This rib runs the length of the barrel.

The Action

The moving parts that permit you to load, fire, and unload your shotgun are known as the action. Most of these parts are housed in a metal frame called a receiver. Many different methods have been designed for operating the action. Among the most common types are bolt, hinge, pump, and semiautomatic. In each case, the ultimate function is the same.

By operating the action, you usually are causing the firing pin to compress. With the action open, a shotshell can be inserted into the chamber at the breech end of the barrel. To open or close the action on many firearms, you must activate the "action release" button or lever.

Loading is done by inserting a shotshell in the chamber of the magazine. After loading, the action is closed and locked. Closing the action on most shotguns means the gun is cocked and ready for firing. This is when you should place the safety in the "on" position. You must then move it to the "off" position right before firing.

Once the gun is cocked and the safety off, the trigger can be pulled when the shotgun has been pointed at the target. Pulling the trigger causes the firing pin to be driven forward. When the firing pin strikes the primer in the base of the shell case, the shotshell will fire.

Reopening the action after the shot is fired will eject the fired case or allow you to remove the fired case by hand. On most shotguns, opening the action will eject the fired case automatically. Then, a new shotshell can be loaded, the action closed, and the gun fired again.

Pump action shotgun and action

Action Types

Pump. The actions of the pump-type shotguns are opened and closed by "pumping" the forearm of the stock back and forth. Pump actions are sometimes called "slide" actions.

Hinge. Similar to the movement of a door hinge, the hinge action can be opened when the release lever on top of the action is pushed to one side. This separates the standing breech block from the barrel. Many shotguns of this type have two barrels. Based on placement, they are referred to as either "over and unders" or "side by sides." They also come with just one barrel and are generally referred to as a "single barrel."

Semiautomatic. This type of action also is appropriately known as autoloading. It operates automatically when the shot is fired. Gas from the burning gunpowder provides the energy needed to operate the action and load the next shell. This type of action delivers less recoil, or "kick," to the shooter.

Bolt. A bolt action shotgun operates in the same lift, pull, and push sequence used in operating a common door bolt. It even looks like one.

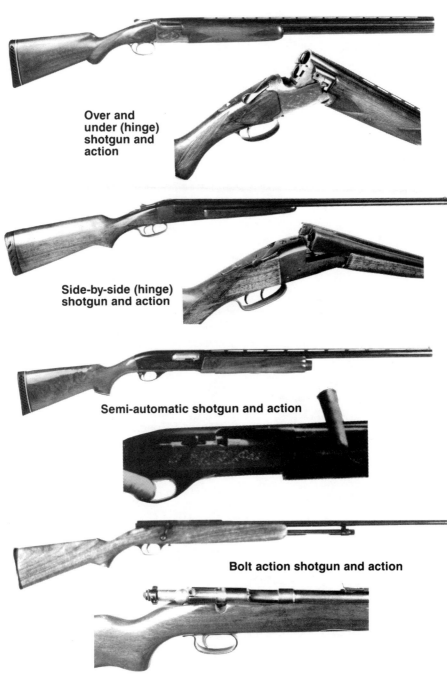

Over and under (hinge) shotgun and action

Side-by-side (hinge) shotgun and action

Semi-automatic shotgun and action

Bolt action shotgun and action

The Magazine

Most shotgun actions can be loaded manually using one shell at a time. Many, however, have a magazine to speed up loading. The magazine is a container attached to the gun into which several shells can be placed. Closing the action on loaded shotguns equipped with a magazine will allow a new shell to be placed in the chamber. The gun can be fired successively until the magazine is empty.

The Basics of Shotgun Shooting

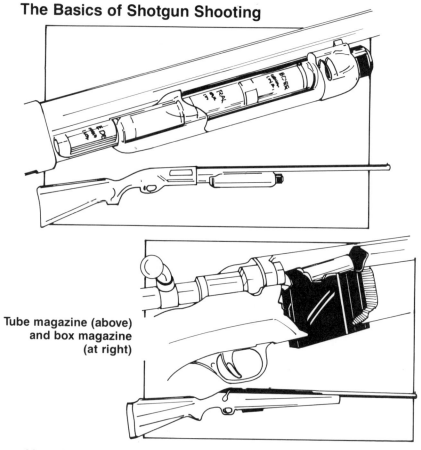

Tube magazine (above) and box magazine (at right)

Magazines are generally of two types. The most common is a tube type positioned under the barrel. The second is a box type located directly under the receiver.

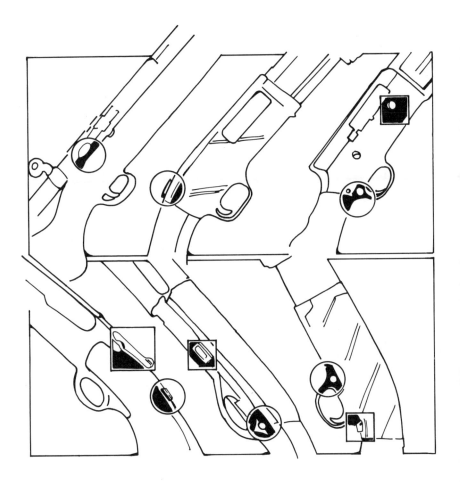

The Safety

Regardless of the type of action employed, most modern shotguns come equipped with a mechanical safety. When the safety is in the "on" position it should prevent the gun from firing. Safeties, as the names imply, help guard against unwanted firing and are normally used when carrying a loaded shotgun.

Under no circumstances should they be used as a substitute for good safety habits. As mechanical devices, safeties are subject to malfunction and forgetfulness by the shooter. Therefore, even when the safety is in the "on" position, the responsible shooter always treats his gun as if firing were possible.

Shotgun Ammunition

The modern shotgun shell contains the five components required for firing the shot. These are the case, primer, powder, wad, and shot.

The Shell Case. This is the outer container for all other ammunition parts. It is typically made of plastic or paper with a metal base.

The Primer. This is contained in the middle of the shell's base where the firing pin will strike.

Shotshell Parts

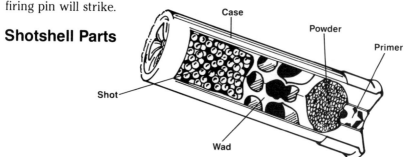

The Powder Charge. This is located above the primer to allow easy combustion from the flame created by the initial detonation of the priming compound.

Fiber Wad. A plastic or fiber wad separates the shot from the powder. It forms a seal allowing the gases created by the burning powder to push the shot down the barrel.

The Shot. Shot are small round projectiles usually made of lead or steel. They are located at the front end of the shell. Depending on the gauge and shot size, a shell may contain anywhere from 9 to 700 of them.

To understand these components, you must understand the way modern firearms work.

Identification Number	SHOT SIZE Shot Diameter	Number of Shot in an Ounce
#9 •	.08	585
#8 •	.09	410
#7½ •	.095	350
#6 •	.11	225
#5 •	.12	170
#4 •	.13	135
#2 •	.15	90

How Shotguns Work

Shotguns "fire" by means of a chain reaction that begins when the trigger is pulled. It ends when the shot are expelled from the barrel. The first step occurs when the trigger is pulled and the firing pin strikes the primer, causing its priming compound to detonate. The flame generated by the

Firing Sequence

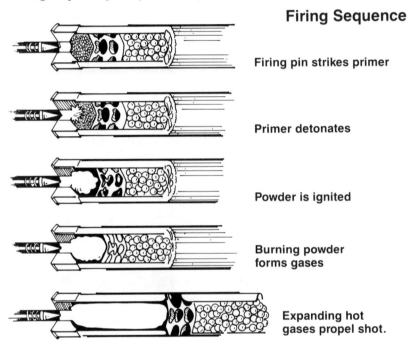

Firing pin strikes primer

Primer detonates

Powder is ignited

Burning powder forms gases

Expanding hot gases propel shot.

primer ignites the powder charge. The rapidly burning powder generates a high volume of gases. Gases under pressure will seek the path of least resistance. The breech end of your shotgun is blocked and the muzzle is open. This path will take the gases through the bore and out the muzzle. In the way of these gases are the wad and shot. But since they give the least resistance, the gases push them along and out the muzzle. All this is done in a split second—at a velocity of 1,250 feet per second. This velocity diminishes as the shot travels until the shot falls to earth at a range of about 300 yards. After 40–60 yards, however, the shot has lost velocity and energy, and the pattern has become so widely dispersed that it isn't possible to hit moving targets.

Using the Right Ammunition

The kind of ammunition you use will depend on the gauge of the gun and the kind of shooting you will do. Use only the shotshells that are right for your shotgun. Usually, modern shotguns are stamped on the barrel to indicate the gauge and the length of the shotshell. The base of the shellcase is also commonly marked with the gauge of the cartridge and its manufacturer. Be sure these match. Ammunition manufacturers usually mark the boxes in which they pack their products with the gauge, shot size, powder charge, and shell length. Buy only the gauge and length appropriate for the gun, and shot size and powder charge suitable for the intended use.

Use the proper gauge of ammunition for your shotgun—take time out to check the identification of box, shells, and shotgun.

Shotgun Safety

The shotgun is a piece of sporting equipment—just like a golf club. Like a golf club, it poses no danger as long as the shooter controlling it knows and follows the safety rules and exercises sound judgment and the common sense required in proper use.

Safe shotgun handling means that every shooter must be 100 percent certain of his gun's status at all times. Safety must be so ingrained that no one with whom you're shooting will ever have to worry about your shotgun. Managing your gun is your job, and your *attitude* must always be one of keeping total control over your firearm. It's not enough just to know the rules of safety. You must always maintain a *positive attitude* towards using them. As you become more and more familiar with firearms, safe handling should become an instinctive habit.

The basic safety rules fall into two categories: those you must observe whenever you are handling your shotgun and those required in the act of shooting.

Basic Rules for Safe Handling

1. Always point the muzzle in a safe direction. Never point the muzzle at yourself or others. Common sense will tell you which direction is safest depending on your location and other conditions. Generally it's safest to point the gun upward or toward the ground.

2. Keep your finger off the trigger until you are ready to shoot. There's a natural tendency to put your finger on the trigger when picking up or handling a gun. Don't do it! Your gun has a trigger guard. It's there to protect your trigger—to enable you to hold the gun comfortably with your finger off the trigger.

3. Keep the action open and your gun unloaded until ready to use. Treat any gun as if it were loaded and ready to go off. Treat every gun as if it were loaded whether at home, on the range, or in the field. This means you never let the gun point at you or anyone else. Whenever you pick up a gun, open the action and check (visually, if possible) to see that the chamber is unloaded. If the gun has a magazine, make sure it's empty. If you don't know how to open the action, leave it alone or get help from someone who's knowledgeable.

Always point the muzzle in a safe direction.

Keep your finger off the trigger.

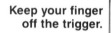

Keep the action open and the gun unloaded.

Remember, even if you're sure that it's not loaded, always point the gun in a safe direction. By handling unloaded guns in the same manner as loaded ones, you're helping establish sound handling habits and will never have to say, "I thought the gun was empty."

But gee, you say, "There are times when I can't follow this exactly. Times like when I have to clean the gun, for example." That's true. There are such times. But remember, an open, empty gun is safe! Open the action and remove the magazine, or be sure it's empty. Be sure the chamber is empty. Leave the action open. When the gun is in this condition it is safe. But the moment you close the action, you must treat the gun as if it were loaded and ready to fire whether or not there's ammunition in it.

Be aware that removing the magazine from the gun does not unload it! Removing the magazine doesn't take the cartridge out of the chamber.

You may want to put your gun away in a cabinet or a gun case. The action will be closed to protect the mechanism. Remember that you always treat the gun as if loaded. To put the gun away in a case, examine the action to be sure it's empty. Point the muzzle in a safe direction, close the action, and pull the trigger. Then put the gun in the cabinet or case—still treating it as a loaded gun.

If a friend asks to look over your gun, there's a simple precaution. You should carefully open the action and examine the chamber and magazine. Show him the interesting features of the shotgun. Explain to him the reasons for keeping the action open and keeping the muzzle pointed in a safe direction. If he wants to handle the shotgun, watch carefully to be sure he handles it safely.

Most of this discussion has centered on using the modern cartridge type of firearm. Additional safety rules apply for the muzzle-loader. It is loaded by putting a measured amount of powder down the muzzle. The shot is also put through the muzzle on top of a wad that separates the powder and shot. Then another wad is inserted to hold all this in place and to add to the compression of the explosion of the powder.

There's no way your eye can tell whether the muzzle-loader is loaded. The best way to determine this is to put the ramrod down through the muzzle when there's no charge in the gun. Make a mark around the ramrod at the muzzle. From this point on, you can tell whether the gun is loaded. Put the ramrod down through the muzzle until it hits bottom. Check the position of the marking on the ramrod. If the mark is above the muzzle, the gun is loaded. Put the gun on half cock and check the nipple to see whether there's a cap in the nipple. If there is, carefully remove it.

If your shotgun is a flintlock and your ramrod test tells you it's loaded, remove all powder from the flash pan. This is the powder lighted by the flint flash.

Rules for Safe Shotgun Shooting

The three principles covered earlier relate to gun handling. There are also rules for safe shooting. When you're actually engaged in shooting—whether in hunting, recreational practice, or competition—the basic rules must always be followed.

1. Know how your shotgun operates. Before handling your gun, learn how it works. This includes knowing the basic parts; how to safely open, load, and close the action; and how to remove any ammunition from the chamber or magazine if it's loaded. Remember, a gun's mechanical safety device is never foolproof. The safety device can never replace safe gun handling.

2. Be sure your shotgun and the ammunition are compatible. Only cartridges or shells designed for a particular gun can be fired in that gun. Most guns have the cartridge or shell type stamped on the barrel. Ammunition can be identified by information printed on the box and stamped on each cartridge. Do not fire the gun if there's any question about the compatibility of the gun and ammunition.

3. Carry only one gauge or caliber of ammunition when shooting. Be sure it's right for the shooting you'll be doing. You'd have trouble hitting a clay pigeon with No. 2 shot instead of No. 9 shot. When you're through shooting, remove unfired ammunition from clothing to avoid accidentally mixing different ammunition the next time you go shooting.

Wear ear and eye protection.

4. Be sure of your target and what's beyond. Be sure you have identified your target without any doubt. Also be sure of the area beyond your target. This means observing your prospective area of fire before you shoot. Never fire in a direction where there are people or any other potential for mishap. It's simple: Think first. Shoot second.

5. Wear eye and ear protection. Guns are loud. They can also emit debris and hot gases that could cause eye injury.

6. Alcohol or drugs don't mix with shooting. They impair normal mental and physical functions. It can be dangerous for you to be near a person who is shooting under the influence of these.

7. Be aware that other conditions may require additional rules. If you plan to go hunting, you'll need to learn the various shotgun carries, how to cross obstacles safely, and much more. Remember, when in your home, at the range, or in the field, you alone are responsible for gun safety.

One last point: On occasion you may run into experienced shooters, or novices unfortunately influenced by them, who have grown careless. A good example of this is the guy who rests the gun muzzle on his toe. This is just plain dumb. Don't be swayed or impressed by such foolishness. If you get into a situation where others refuse to follow the safety rules—don't shoot with them.

Cleaning Your Shotgun

Your shotgun is a piece of precision equipment. Like any item of value, it must be given proper care if it's to operate correctly and safely. Unlike many items of sports equipment, your shotgun is built to last a lifetime. And it will if you regularly care for it.

Ideally, you should make a habit of cleaning your shotgun each time it is used. A gun that is cleaned regularly will shoot more accurately and reliably. Cleaning also preserves the finish and value of the shotgun. Cleaning is also needed when the shotgun has been stored for an extended period, or has been exposed to dirt or moisture. Don't start shooting with a dirty gun. Be sure it's cleaned thoroughly before use.

As you begin to clean your shotgun, first make sure the action is open and all ammunition removed. To assure absolute safety, always keep the action open during cleaning.

Six basic materials are needed to clean a gun that fires by cartridge or gunpowder. These are:

- Cleaning rod with attachments to hold patches (these must be the proper size for the bore of the gun).

- Cloth patches, available commercially or made at home from absorbent cloth, to remove foreign particles from the barrel's interior surface and to apply solvent or lubricant.

- Bore-cleaning solvent that dissolves powder residue.

- Light gun oil to apply to the moving parts of the gun. Check the manufacturer's recommendation.

- A clean cloth to clean the exterior parts of the gun. The cloth should be free of dirt and moisture.

- A small brush like a toothbrush for cleaning the nooks and crannies on your gun.

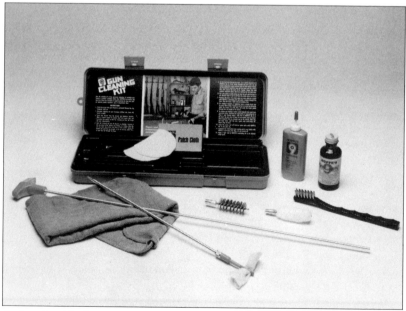

A cleaning kit should include cleaning rod, attachments, cleaning patches, bore solvent, brush, gun oil and a clean cloth

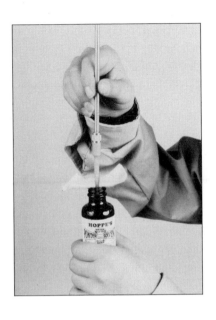

Steps in Cleaning

1. Place a cleaning patch on the cleaning rod, wet with cleaning solvent, and work it back and forth in the bore to loosen residue and fouling. If the bore is very dirty, substitute a brass or bronze cleaning brush and repeat the brushing until most of the residue is loosened. Then repeat with a moistened patch.

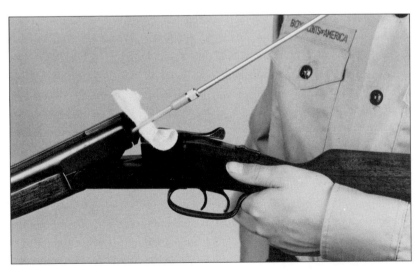

2. Thoroughly dry the bore by repeating the above process, using three or four clean, dry patches. Continue until a patch comes through clean after running the length of the barrel.

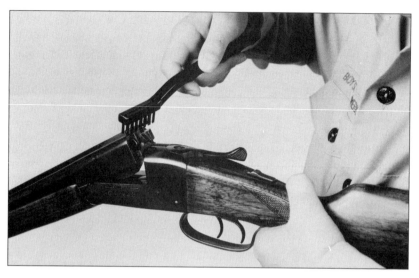

3. Wipe all the exterior parts of the gun with a clean cloth, being particularly careful to remove any accumulated grease or dirt from the gun's moving parts. This is where the toothbrush will be needed.

4. Check all removable parts of your gun—including stock, screws, magazine, tube cap, and similar parts—to be sure they are all fastened tightly.

5. After all the metallic surfaces have been cleaned and dried, protect them during storage by wiping down with a clean cloth lightly moistened with gun oil. Don't foreget the inside of the bore and chamber. Don't overdo it! A light coat of lubricant will be enough.

Gun Repairs

Don't try to repair any part of your shotgun that appears to be malfunctioning or broken. At this point in your shooting career, even the most minor repairs should be left to an expert. There's a simple reason for this. With your minimal knowledge, any improper repair could cause your gun to fire improperly or cause further damage—with potentially hazardous results. At the least, you could irreparably damage your shotgun. Don't take chances. Take your shotgun to an experienced gunsmith and let him solve your problem.

Transporting Your Shotgun

State and local regulations vary. You must make it your business to learn what laws apply where you live, at points in transit, and at your destination. Some places have ordinances restricting firearm transport. Part of your obligation as a responsible shooter is to know and comply with the laws. To obtain information about laws in your area, contact your local law enforcement agency or the National Rifle Association, Research and Information Department.

Sensible Storage

Before you decide how and where you are going to keep your gun or guns and ammunition, consider safety, storage conditions, access by others, and your personal needs. Many people are intrigued by guns, and the temptation to pick one up is very real for adults and children alike. That could spell trouble if the person is too young or inexperienced to handle the gun safely. Security is another factor. Unfortunately, guns are often desirable booty for thieves.

For all these reasons, it's wise to find a secure and convenient location for your shooting equipment. Many manufacturers offer fine wooden cabinets to display and secure your gun or guns. Some gun owners prefer to have their guns in locked metal vaults or storage places where they are out of sight and out of reach. If you choose storage that requires a lock, be sure to keep your keys in a place where casual visitors and youngsters aren't likely to find them.

Ammunition should be kept in a cool, dry place. Many gun owners prefer to store their ammunition separately from their guns to minimize the chance of an accident.

There are many areas of safety and protection not covered here. Think about a few examples and what you could do about them. For example, when hunting in the field, you come to a fence. How can you and your gun get safely to the other side? Remember to deactivate your gun as the first step. Open the action and remove all ammunition. Place your gun carefully on the ground under the lower wire or rail of the fence. Then walk to a fencepost away from your gun. Climb the fence and cross to the other side. Then carefully pick up your gun in such a way that the muzzle is never aimed at you. Now you can put the ammunition back in the gun and continue hunting.

Fundamentals of Shotgun Shooting

Learning to shoot is like mastering any other skill. No first-day skier would venture to the top of the peak for his first run. Nor should you, as a first-time shooter, begin by loading up and blasting away at targets flying in every direction.

Your introduction should start with an understanding of what must be accomplished in the process of learning and using basic skills to hit the target. We'll begin with a discussion of the fundamentals of shotgun shooting. Five steps are involved. We refer to them as "fundamentals" because they must be practiced and adhered to in exact sequence every time you take a shot. Once you've learned the fundamentals, you can begin to apply them to a variety of shotgunning sports. The five fundamentals are: (1) Shooting position (stance), (2) shot preparation (gun-ready position), (3) swing to target, (4) trigger pull, and (5) follow-through.

Before you start learning these fundamentals, there's an important question you must answer about yourself. On which side should you shoulder your gun? Whether you're right- or left-handed isn't as important as which eye is dominant.

You may not be conscious of it, but you probably have one eye that's dominant over the other. Since the ability to align your shotgun with a moving target is essential, you should use your dominant eye and shoulder your gun on that side. How do you determine this? There's an easy test: Extend your hands in front of your face, placing them together so that only a small opening remains between them. Now look through this space, focusing on some distant object.

While maintaining your focus, keep both eyes open and start moving your hands closer to your face. Continue this motion until your hands reach your face. At this point, you will have instinctively lined up the opening in your hands with one eye. That's your dominant eye.

Shooting Position (Stance)

Almost every shot you'll make with a shotgun is from the standing position, so learn it well. Your shooting position must be relaxed and comfortable. This means attaining a stance that's as natural a balance as possible without straining your muscles. Your feet should be about shoulder width apart and planted firmly on the ground. Your front knee should be bent slightly while your back leg remains straight. This position provides proper balance and the ability to move.

Aligning your shooting position with the expected target-breaking area is the second essential consideration. This position will let you easily rotate your body if the target moves to the right or left.

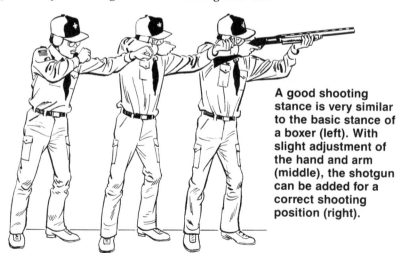

A good shooting stance is very similar to the basic stance of a boxer (left). With slight adjustment of the hand and arm (middle), the shotgun can be added for a correct shooting position (right).

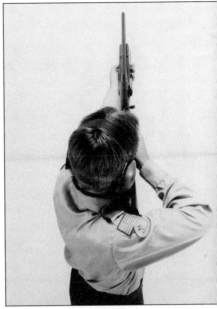

Line up stance with expected target breaking area (left).

With a shotgun added, you can move quickly to the target (right).

Shot Preparation (Gun Ready Position)

This is the position you hold while waiting for the target to appear. It is intended to make your "swing to the target" as easy as possible. Maintain your basic shooting stance. Hold the shotgun with your nontrigger hand at about the middle of the shotgun forearm. Your grip should be firm, but not so tight as to create strain. The same is true of your trigger hand placed on the grip of the stock.

A gun ready position is relaxed and enhances your ability to see the target area.

29

Place the muzzle just below the anticipated target's flight path to allow a clear view of target—Keep both eyes open.

The rear position of the stock is positioned along the front side of your ribs. The muzzle is placed slightly below the expected flight path of the target. This provides a clear view of the target area. Both eyes should be open, and focused in the area where you expect the target will first appear.

Swing to Target

On first seeing the target, move your gun and body as a single coordinated unit toward the target, raising the gun into the correct firing position. To achieve this position:

- Keep your eyes focused on the target all the time.

- Bring the stock to the face. It should be firmly in place against the face.

- Bring the trigger hand elbow into position about level with the shoulders.

- Place the butt of the stock against the shoulder.

A good shooting position—study it!

Keep comb of stock firmly in position against cheek of face.

With correct gun fit, the barrel will be aligned in front of your dominant eye and with the target. The swing to target must be done quickly, in a smooth and fluid movement. It's important to note that unlike lining up the sights of a rifle, sighting is more of a pointing motion with your shotgun.

Trigger Pull

Timing and reflex are essential in the act of trigger pull. The trigger pull should take place at the instant when, looking at the moving target, you see your gun's muzzle touch it. Your pull must be quick and crisp.

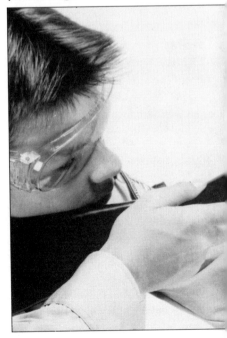

Follow-through

This is one of the most important and difficult aspects of shotgun shooting. The shotgun muzzle must move through the target if the shots are to hit the target. The trigger is pulled while the shotgun is moving, and the gun must continue to move after the shot is fired. The shotgun must remain welded to your body, and especially the cheek. Stopping the motion of the gun after touching the target is the most common cause of misses by beginning shotgunners. Always continue to keep the gun moving by following through!

Knowing the fundamentals is the foundation of successful shooting. Using them correctly and consistently every time provides successful shooting whether you're a beginner or an expert. As you're about to discover, the steps involved in actual shooting are methodical, progressive, and equally vital.

Firing Your First Shots

You're about to begin a multistep process. The most effective way to produce the desired results is to be patient and take it a step at a time. Only after proper preparation and review is the shotgun and then the ammunition added. The rewards will come when you find your shots hitting the target rather than thin air.

Know Your Target

In the exercises to come, you'll be building up to your first shots firing on airborne targets thrown by hand or a mechanical trap. First, let's look at the target.

The breakable clay target is excellent for learning and is used by millions in target competition. Clay targets are readily available at most sporting goods stores. Some gun clubs and ranges may provide them for their participants. They are easily thrown with a mechanical trap and cost very little.

Learn everything you can about the target. Handle it and see how easily it breaks. Observe how its design facilitates flight much like a Frisbee. Watch several in flight. On the range, you will notify the trap operator that you want a target thrown with the command "Pull." Notice how the target emerges from the trap when it is ejected. Get the feel for how fast and where the target flies.

Start with a Straightaway Target

You'll notice that accomplished shooters fire from many different positions and with targets coming or going from many different directions, angles,

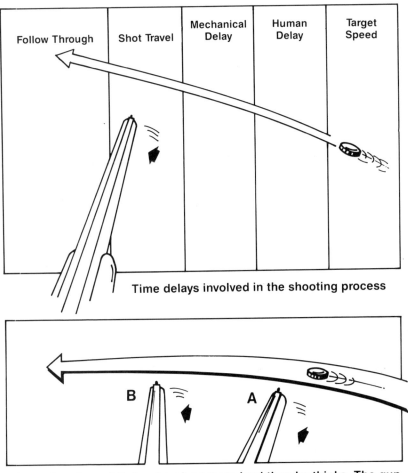

Follow Through	Shot Travel	Mechanical Delay	Human Delay	Target Speed

Time delays involved in the shooting process

The "swing through" shooter gives more lead than he thinks. The gun barrel (A) shows where he thinks he shoots on a crossing target. The barrel (B) is where he really shoots if a good follow through is used.

speeds, and distances. But, at the start, you should practice on targets flying in only one direction.

The trap is set so that it will throw the target fairly straightaway in front of you. Initially, each target should follow virtually the same flight path and travel at a relatively slow speed. The background against which the target will be thrown should be clear—an open sky with a low horizon line and no obstructions is ideal. All of this enhances your ability to concentrate and focus on the target—and hit it.

Learn to Point

Before you actually start working with your shotgun, it's a good idea to run through the fundamentals with a target, using your index finger as a substitute for the shotgun itself. This exercise will teach you to point toward the flying target without having to concentrate on the body movements required to position the shotgun. This will enhance your ability to concentrate on the target at all times.

Assume the proper stance, but with your index finger pointed at a 45-degree angle to the ground. Line up your stance with the expected target-breaking area. If your right eye is dominant, point with your left hand. If it's your left eye, point with the right hand. By doing this, when the time comes to add the shotgun, your shooting position will be correct. Now focus your eyes on the area where your target will first appear and call "Pull."

As soon as you see your target, immediately move your finger to the target and keep your finger aligned with it until it hits the ground. Practice this motion several times. Look at the target all the time, not the finger you are pointing with. This is an important concept in shotgun shooting—shotguns are pointed, not aimed. The difference is that your eyes must always remain focused on the target, never on the shotgun barrel or beads.

When you begin to be familiar with this pointing exercise, add a sound effect. When the target is released, again move your finger to it smoothly. At the instant your finger seems to touch the target, simulate pulling the trigger by saying "Bang!" Remember to follow through. This may sound a bit too much like kid stuff for your tastes. There's a distinct purpose for this. In shotgun shooting, it's imperative to be able to time your shot so that you pull the trigger as soon as the muzzle seems to touch the target. By saying "Bang," you are learning to recognize and develop a mental picture of actions in shooting that should eventually become instinctive.

Practice Pointing With Your Shotgun

Now you can start using the gun itself. Remember all the basic safety rules. Keep the muzzle pointed in a safe direction and keep your finger off the trigger until you're ready to shoot. Check to make sure both the chamber and the magazine are unloaded by opening the action and making sure no shells are in the gun.

Your first step with the shotgun in your hands should be to review the first three shooting fundamentals. Get into the proper shooting position.

Make sure your stance is balanced and allows you to easily rotate from right to left and back, covering the shooting area. Assume the gun ready position. Now practice bringing the shotgun from the gun ready position into the correct firing position. Check to be sure you're doing everything "according to the book." Take your time—practice.

Once you've learned to bring the shotgun smoothly into the correct firing position, it's time to add the target. Practice calling for and swinging to the target, following it all the way to the ground. This teaches you to stay with your gun. Be sure your eyes remain focused on the target all the time.

Dry-firing

After working on the first three fundamentals, you can add pulling the trigger—with the action closed but unloaded. This is called dry-firing. After checking the chamber and magazine, close the action, place the safety in the "off" position, and assume your stance and gun ready position. Now call "Pull," this time pulling the trigger the instant your muzzle sight touches the target.

Now's the time to really work on follow-through. Doing everything exactly the same as when you pulled the trigger, practice staying with the gun for 2 or 3 seconds after firing. Remember to keep the stock firmly in place against your cheek. Open the action after each shot, just as if you were really ejecting a spent shell.

Shooting Live Ammunition

When you've dry-fired a number of times, it's time to start shooting with live ammunition. You will need to return your gun to the rack to get prepared. Start with a review of firearm handling and shooting rules. Make sure you know them and follow them! Put on your eye and ear protectors. Get no more than five rounds of ammunition, pick up your shotgun, and move to the firing station.

From here on it's a good idea to learn to do each step by the numbers. Learning to do the steps the same way every time is the key to consistent success in shooting. Follow these seven steps:

1. Move to station, load appropriate number of shells (in this case, one), and place the gun's safety in the "off" position.

2. Establish stance in relation to target area.

3. Establish gun ready position with muzzle slightly below the target flight path. Place your finger on the trigger.

4. Focus your eyes on the target area where the target will appear.

5. Call "Pull" for target.

6. On seeing target, swing to target, pull trigger, and follow through.

7. Open action and unload shotgun immediately after firing.

How did you do? If you followed the fundamentals, you should have broken a target. If your untouched target dropped to the ground, don't be too hard on yourself. This is just the first shot of many eventful days of shooting to come. As in all sports requiring skill and coordination, successful shotgun shooting means ongoing practice. So try again! As you refine your ability to concentrate on the target, you'll begin to see targets breaking one after the other.

Practice with straightaway targets until you hit them fairly consistently. Then you can move on to more difficult targets by gradually changing their angles of flight.

Scoring

Your cartridge-type shotgun shooting will be done using a gun in the range of 12 gauge, 16 gauge, 20 gauge, 28 gauge, or .410 caliber. You should use a gun well-fitted and light enough to eliminate unwanted movement when shooting.

You will be shooting at clay targets thrown by a hand trap, mechanical trap, or on any trap or skeet field. The trap operator shall be at least 5 feet to the right and 3 feet to the rear of the shooter. If throwing left-handed with a hand trap, this should be reversed.

You will shoot in rounds of 25. Rounds need not be shot consecutively or on the same day. (The term "round" refers to a single series of 25 shots).

To score with a cartridge-type shotgun, you must hit at least 24 (48 percent) out of 50 targets (two 25-target rounds). To score with the muzzle-loader, you must hit at least 5 out of 15 targets.

With the muzzle-loader, you are also permitted to fire with a 10-gauge shotgun if you are capable of handling that big a gun.

Choosing a Shotgun

Getting a shotgun of your own can be something you'll remember all of your life. But picking the right one can be tough. The larger the bore, the heavier the shotgun will be. This makes the .410 shotgun the lightest, and the 10-gauge shotgun the heaviest. You'll certainly want a shotgun that you are capable of handling and that will do the job for which it's intended. A 12-gauge will give an effective shot density for a beginner and a gas-operated system (autoloader) will reduce recoil.

Study available guns in your area. You might start at your local library, where you'll find books showing most of the firearms for sale in the country. A visit to a sporting goods or gun speciality store is a must. Here, you can handle the various guns and test their "feel." Find a truly interested salesperson to explain the features of the models you're studying. Be specific about your interests, plans for use, and budget. Take your time. Don't buy on impulse or a quick sales pitch.

Select a Shotgun That Fits

The main part of a shotgun's fit is in the stock. Most manufacturers sell shotguns with standard stock dimensions designed to fit the average-size

This youngster has a shotgun that was specifically designed and manufactured for young people. Trying to use dad's shotgun (left) just doesn't work.

adult. Many also produce youth models with smaller or adjustable dimensions suitable to a smaller physique.

There are two important fit considerations—the length and the comb of the stock. For young people or adults with short arms or stature, standard length stocks are usually too long.

You can measure the fit by placing the butt in the crook of your arm. Your hand should comfortably reach the pistol grip and trigger. If the stock is too long, it's possible for a gunsmith to refit the gun for your size. But this shouldn't be necessary with a new gun. You should be able to buy a gun that fits. Only in picking up a second-hand gun might you want to have it fitted by a gunsmith.

- How do you plan to use this shotgun? Will it be mainly for shooting at clay targets or will you also want to hunt in the field? What is the best gauge for this?

- Is ammunition readily available? How much will it cost for the amount of shooting you'll do?

- How much do you have, or how much can you spend for a shotgun?

- Have you done your homework? Have you studied manufacturers' catalogs? Have you looked at and handled different makes available?

- Is the shotgun simple to operate and easy to clean?

- Does the gun fit you?

- Some manufacturers make shotguns designed for use from the left shoulder.

- Have you read the warranty or guarantees?

- Is the shotgun produced by a known manufacturer? Buying quality brands will generally ensure the availability of future repairs and parts. It will help bring a good return on your investment.

- Does the shotgun have a good record for dependability?

- Are you purchasing from a reputable dealer who'll be around when needed?

- What is the marketability if you decide to sell your shotgun? Could you get back most of your investment if you sell?

- Have you taken your time in making your choice?

    Remember, chances are good you'll keep your shotgun for life.

When you pull the gun into the shooting position, your cheek should sit tightly against the comb, and the barrel should be directly in front of your dominant shooting eye.

If the shotgun fits, this is the view you should get when looking down the barrel.

Before You Buy

Check out these questions before you make your choice. Your answers will guide you and prevent a hasty decision.

Buying a Used Shotgun

If you're shopping for a used gun, consider these points:

- Locate the previous owner, if possible, and find out why the shotgun was traded or sold.

- A poor outward appearance of a shotgun generally indicates abuse or excessive wear.

- Make certain a reblue or refinish job hasn't disguised past use of the shotgun.

- Check screw slots to see that they haven't been abused during disassembly or by an inexperienced person.

- Check the trigger for consistent, safe pull and smooth function. Check the safety to be sure it functions properly.

- Note that shotguns in an original, unaltered condition tend to be of more value.

- Get advice from an expert on guns regarding this shotgun's market value.

- Check the wood in the stock for type, quality, and hairline cracks.

- Shoot the shotgun, if possible, before buying.

- Be certain the shotgun is legally owned by the seller.

- You usually get what you pay for! Beware of deals that are too good to be true—they usually are.

Olympic Games and Shooting

Olympic-style shooting evolved from the European tradition. It is characterized by uniform courses of fire and strict regulations governing clothing, equipment, and firearms to ensure the uniformity of these items used in international competition.

Shooting is governed worldwide by the International Shooting Union (UIT), with headquarters in Munich, West Germany. The National Rifle Association of America is recognized by the U.S. Olympic Committee as the national governing body for the shooting sports in this country.

The shotgun sports fired in the Olympics are:

International Trap

This event is an open event, meaning men and women compete equally. Competitors fire a 12-gauge shotgun at breakable clay targets flying at speeds of up to 110 miles per hour. The match is fired over a 15-trap bunker layout, or over an automatic "wobble" trap. Either system throws the clay discs a minimum of 70 meters (77 yards) at random angles and elevations. Shooters fire at 25 targets, making their way around a series of five stations in a straight line behind the trap house. Each station has a voice-activated microphone beside it, allowing for instant target release when the competitor calls for the target. Shooters fire a total of five shots from each station, moving to the next station after each shot. Competitors mount their shotguns on their shoulders before calling for the target. Shooters are allowed two shots per target. The angle of the target is never known until it appears, building elements of excitement and difficulty into this sport.

Course of fire: 200 targets in eight rounds of 25. Targets may be shot in 2 days at 100 targets each day or in 3 days at 75 + 75 + 50 targets.

Perfect score: 200

Target: Fast-moving, breakable clay targets measuring 4½ inches in diameter and shaped like small Frisbees

International Skeet

This also is an open event, fired with a 12-gauge shotgun at targets traveling nearly 110 miles per hour. Shooters may fire only one shot per target. Targets are thrown by mechanical traps a minimum distance of 65 meters (71.5 yards). The targets are breakable clay discs, identical to those used in trap. The clay targets are thrown from one or both of two buildings on the far right and left of the skeet field. On the left is the high house, throwing targets about eight feet from ground level. Shooters fire from eight stations placed in a semicircle facing a line between the two houses. Unlike international trap, the starting position of skeet requires the competitor to hold the shotgun at hip level until the target appears. Only then may the shotgun be raised to the shoulder. The difficulty of this sport is enhanced by the variable time release of the targets, allowing for a 0–3 second delay from the time the shooter calls for the target until it appears.

Course of fire: 200 targets in eight rounds of 25. May be shot in 2 days at 100 targets per day or in 3 days at 75 + 75 + 50 targets.

Perfect score: 200

Target: Breakable clay discs made of limestone and pitch, each measuring 4½ inches in diameter

For additional information, write to:

NRA Shooting Sports
U.S. Olympic Training Center
1750 East Boulder Street
Colorado Springs, CO 80909

Conservation and Hunting

Wildlife biologists have long recognized that there are two major factors in game management.

The first is that you can't stockpile wildlife. With few exceptions, a given piece of ground can support only a given number of one type of wildlife. If you decide you'd like to have more game of a certain kind in that area, and you stock it with additional wildlife, what will happen? If you go back in a year or so, you won't find any increase in the number of animals. Starvation, disease, or predators will have taken the extra ones.

The second factor of importance is that nature overproduces every year, producing far more animals than the area can support. The excess is lost. It is nature's way of making sure that there are enough animals each year for breeding, and for ensuring that only the strongest survive for reproduction. For example, only 8 percent of young rabbits grow to the breeding stage. If you start with 100 pheasant eggs in June, there will be 50 chicks by the first of October but fewer than 10 birds left by the following May.

These principles apply despite what you do to the animals. If you put extra birds or small animals in the area, they will die. If you kill extra birds or small animals, the remaining stock will soon bring the population up to the normal figure. Wildlife management experts try to arrange hunting seasons and bag limits so that any surplus can be harvested by hunters. Hunting regulations ensure that hunters do not take too many animals. Far better that the hunter should get the healthful outdoor recreation—and the meat—harvesting the surplus than to lose it to disease, starvation, and other natural causes.

Occasionally, an animal population will grow too large. For a few years there will be a larger carryover than the land can support properly. When it is obvious that the carryover is too large, it is important to increase the harvest and get the numbers down to a safe size for the land. Game managers will often increase the length of hunting seasons and increase the bag limit to do this. Hunters harvest game that would otherwise be lost to natural causes. They help nature bring an excess down to a safe size.

The real problem for game birds and animals is what man has done and is doing to the habitat in which they live. Replacing woods, fields, and marshes with subdivisions, shopping centers, superhighways, industrial complexes, or airports leads to reduced numbers of game birds and animals.

Hunting Regulations

Each state has its own hunting regulations. These are usually listed by the state fish and game department, conservation department, or some similar branch of government that controls hunting and fishing. You can obtain copies of the regulations by writing to the correct department at your state capital. Locally, you can usually get these from a sporting goods store or hardware store where hunting licenses are sold. Your merit badge counselor can help you with this, too.

There are many differences in state game laws. Hunting in Kansas is unlike hunting in California or New York. Differences in geography, population, and game types call for different game laws. Even within a certain state there will be differences in some game laws. Certain areas or counties may have different regulations because of local conditions. Federal regulations cover migratory birds such as ducks. You need a federal migratory bird hunting and conservation stamp to hunt them.

In shotgun hunting language, "birds" are flying critters like grouse, partridge, pheasant, ducks, and geese. "Small game" usually includes rabbits, raccoons, opossums, squirrels, and the like.

Some types of wildlife are considered undesirable, and there are no regulations on hunting them in many states. Included are such animals as the crow, the ground squirrel, and the gopher.

While most game birds and animals don't travel far from where they were born, ducks, geese, doves, and a few other species travel hundreds or thousands of miles. As a result, state game laws are ineffective in controlling the harvest of this game even within the boundaries of the United States. Mexico, the United States, and Canada cooperate to control the hunting of these migratory game birds.

Many states have regulations regarding the use or carrying of guns when hunting. These are designed to protect you and others in the hunting neighborhood. Such laws might prohibit carrying a loaded gun in a car, shooting from a car, or shooting near buildings. Many states control the type of gun that can be used for some kinds of hunting.

Most states require hunters to carry a hunting license. This licensing controls the game harvest, and the fees provide funds for development and game management. To get your hunting license for the first time, many states require the new hunter to satisfactorily complete a hunter safety course. Initially developed by the National Rifle Association and now controlled by each state's hunter education program, these courses are given by volunteer instructors. Even if your state doesn't require you to take such a course, it's certainly worth your time to take it before you start hunting. You'll find it interesting, and if you've earned your Shotgun Shooting merit badge, you won't find it too difficult.

Sportsmanship

Sportsmanship is basic to hunting safety and to conservation. The true sportsman follows the Golden Rule. He treats others the way he would like to have them treat him.

The sportsman knows and always follows the rules for safe gun handling at home, on the range, and in the field. He knows and strictly follows the laws regarding possession and use of firearms. The sportsman knows and strictly follows the rules and regulations of competitive shooting. He knows and follows the letter and spirit of the hunting regulations.

The sportsman is considerate of the landowner whose property he may be using. He asks permission to hunt on the property. He leaves gates as he finds them. He is careful not to damage fences or other property. He doesn't litter the area with trash.

The accomplishment of taking game during the hunt is only part of the experience. Enjoying the outdoors, seeing wildlife, and stalking game are also pleasurable parts of the hunt.

The sportsman is careful of his target, not only for safety but to avoid senseless destruction. He doesn't shoot powerline insulators, pipeline valves, signs, or similar property. He confines his shots to proper targets.

The sportsman is careful of the area beyond his target to ensure that shot pellets that miss the target or ricochet don't travel on to cause damage.

The sportsman doesn't take unfair advantage of another shooter in any way.

Muzzle-loading Shotguns

Until the introduction of cartridge firearms in the 1800s, all firearms were muzzle-loaders. The firearm originated more than 500 years ago. Its inventors found that when a highly combustible material was confined and then lighted, the resulting burning or explosion created enough energy to send a projectile over long distances.

The earliest firearms were incredibly crude and unpredictable by today's standards. Since their inception, firearms have consisted of three basic parts: the lock (or firing mechanism known today as the action), the stock (the handle by which the gun is held), and the barrel (the hollow tube through which the projectile travels on its way to the target).

The term muzzle-loader comes from the fact that all of these guns were loaded through the muzzle.

First came the matchlock, a gun fired by a lighted wick that ignited the powder. This was followed by the wheel lock. This gun's powder was ignited by a spark that came from a wheel spinning against flint. Then came the flintlock and the percussion lock. These are the two that are considered in this merit badge pamphlet.

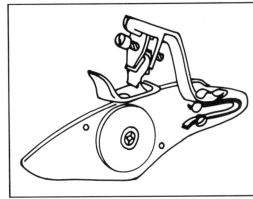

Wheel lock

Matchlock

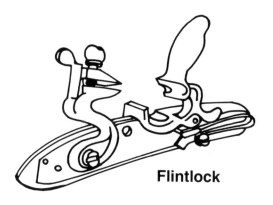

Flintlock

The flintlock was developed in the 1600s. A piece of flint was secured between the jaws of the cock, or hammer as it is commonly called. The priming powder was contained in a pan, covered by a hinged lid. This is the frizzen. When the trigger was pulled, the flint struck a metal arm that was the upright portion of the frizzen. As the flint scraped the frizzen face, sparks flew into the priming charge in the frizzen pan.

The final advance in the history of the muzzle-loader took place in the early 1800s. During this era, a compound called fulminate of mercury began to replace powder as the priming agent. This compound was housed in a small metal container known as a percussion cap. When the cap was struck by the hammer of the gun, it ignited, setting off the powder charge. Percussion caps were the forerunner of the modern cartridge. They represented the first use of a prepackaged priming agent in the firing mechanism.

The first two examples of the early muzzle-loaders are found today only in museums or in the hands of collectors. The last two, the flintlock and the percussion lock, are alive and well. There are relics of the Civil War still being fired today. The popularity of these two guns is great enough for manufacturers to make replicas that can be found in sporting goods stores.

The muzzle-loading shotgun developed from the old smoothbore rifle. All that was needed to make a shotgun out of the smoothbore was some small shot and wadding to hold the shot in place. This replaced the lead ball of the smoothbore rifle.

Parts of the Muzzle-loading Shotgun

You've heard the expression "lock, stock, and barrel." In today's language this expression means the job is finished. Actually, it's an old expression coming from the parts of a muzzle-loader.

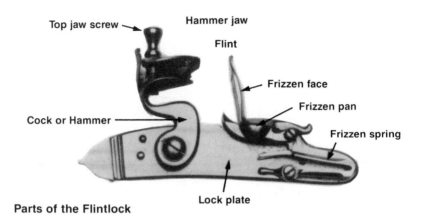

Top jaw screw

Hammer jaw

Flint

Frizzen face

Frizzen pan

Cock or Hammer

Frizzen spring

Lock plate

Parts of the Flintlock

The Lock

This is the portion of the gun used to ignite the main charge in the barrel. The lock will differ depending on whether it's for flintlock or percussion lock. In the flintlock, certain steps must be taken to ensure that the flint can be activated properly. The jaws of the hammer on these firearms generally contain a bed of leather or thin lead that holds the flint firmly yet cushions it to prevent breakage. In positioning the flint, you must not allow the front edge to touch the closed frizzen when the hammer is in the half-cock position. The position you select for inserting the flint will depend on what

The percussion shotgun is the most common version of muzzle-loading shotguns used by muzzle-loaders today.

Parts of the percussion lock

works best with your gun. The bevel (slant) of the flint may be either up or down—whichever is more successful.

The action of pulling the trigger trips the lock. In this process, the hammer comes down briskly, striking the face of the frizzen or percussion cap and setting off the ignition necessary to fire the main powder charge. The percussion gun has a small cap that can be fitted over the nipple. When the hammer strikes the cap it detonates, sending the ignition down to the main powder charge. It's important that you understand the workings of the mechanism for either gun, since this knowledge will be helpful in caring for and cleaning your gun.

The Stock

This is the part by which the gun is held. It is particularly important in muzzle-loading guns. Shotguns fire with some backward recoil, or kick. Thus the butt must be designed so that it fits snugly against your shoulder to absorb these forces. The end of the stock that makes contact with your shoulder is called the butt. The top portion of the butt is called the heel, and the bottom portion the toe.

Aiming the shotgun also brings the stock into play. Since the sighting features on a shotgun are quite basic, bringing the gun into position where the eye has a clear view of the target and its projected path is essential. In such a position the shooter's cheek touches the stock in a top area known as the comb. The "fit" of a shotgun stock to a particular shooter is an essential part of accurate shooting.

The stock must be designed to allow the shooter to grip the entire gun firmly. The portion of the stock grasped by the hand in order to pull the trigger is known, appropriately, as the grip. Yet another purpose of the stock is to provide a firm support for the barrel. The part of the stock extending under the barrel is known as the fore-end.

The Barrel

Shotgun barrels have a smooth bore. The diameter of shotgun bores commonly varies from ½ inch to more than ¾ inch. The term used to describe the bore of a shotgun is called the gauge. The most common bore sizes of muzzle-loading shotguns are 10, 12, 16, 20, and 28 gauge.

Unlike breech-loading shotguns, most muzzle-loading shotguns have little or no choke. Choke is the term used to describe the narrowing of the barrel at the last several inches nearest the muzzle. The more the barrel is choked, the less the pattern spreads.

Choke is unusual in muzzle-loading shotguns because the smaller choked portion makes it difficult to load a bore-size wad through the muzzle. As a result, muzzle-loading shot patterns tend to be wider than those of most breech-loading guns.

The rear end of the muzzle is called the breech end. It is closed by a breech plug that is screwed into it.

Since the shot is spread wider on the muzzle-loader, these guns are generally used more in hunting or shooting moving targets. The sighting apparatus tends to be simple. Muzzle-loading shotguns usually have a small bead attached to the top of the barrel at the muzzle end. Your eye then serves as the rear sight. This is why proper positioning of the stock in the act of shooting is so vital. Actually, a shotgun is pointed and not aimed.

Using Black Powder

True "black powder" is essentially the same substance that has been used as ammunition in muzzle-loaders for centuries. It's a mixture of saltpeter (potassium nitrate), charcoal, and sulfur that, when burned, emits a dense cloud of white smoke. It was first developed for use as a propellant in rock throwing around 1200 A.D., and has remained essentially unchanged over the past 800 years.

Regardless of any information you may receive to the contrary, only sporting-grade black powder or a designated substitute such as Pyrodex can be safely used in muzzle-loading guns. Take no chances in making your

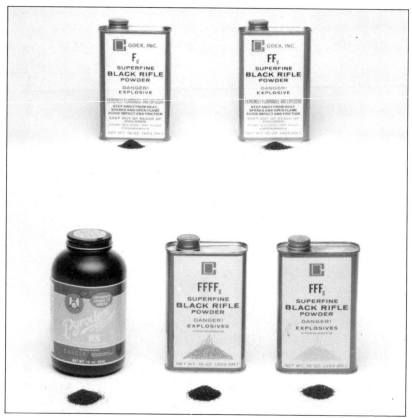

Clockwise from top left: Fg powder, FFg powder, FFFg powder, FFFFg powder and Pyrodex brand substitute black powder

selection. Deal with a reputable firm and make sure the substance you are buying is commercially manufactured and intended for use in muzzle-loaders.

Black powder usable in muzzle-loading firearms can be found in four granulations. The grain size of the powder will determine its rate of burning. The finer the grain, the faster the powder will burn and, therefore, the greater the pressure it will develop. Under containment this pressure increases greatly. The very finest black powder should never be used as the main charge.

The four basic granulations are:

- Fg   Coarse-grain powder used in shotguns of 10 gauge and larger.

- FFg   Medium-grain powder used in shotguns of 10–20 gauge.

- FFFg   Fine-grained powder used in shotguns smaller than 20 gauge.

- FFFFg   This extra fine-grain powder should be used only as a priming agent (never as the main powder charge) in flintlocks.

Pyrodex is available from a number of sources. Although its chemical makeup is different from that of black powder, when used in equal amounts it will produce about the same pressure, bullet velocity, smoke, and noise as black powder. Pyrodex is not recommended for use with flintlocks because of difficulty in ignition. Loading procedures for Pyrodex may vary. Your gun dealer or manufacturer should be able to provide details.

Whether you are using black powder or Pyrodex, you must exercise proper safety. Both are explosives, and as such are subject to rapid and unexpected ignition unless treated with utmost caution in handling. You must also check local ordinances pertaining to the storage of explosives of this nature. Laws vary, and you have full responsibility to respect and obey whatever conditions are applicable in your community. When using black powder or Pyrodex:

- Always store in a safe container. Black powder usually comes in a 1-pound metal can. This is an excellent container for protecting the powder against sparks or heat. Make sure the can is firmly sealed when not in use. Never store black powder in a glass or plastic container.

- Always handle powder in an open, well-ventilated area. In the process of pouring powder in the powder horn or flask you use for transporting in the field, you can accumulate fine powder dust that can easily ignite if put in contact with a spark, flame, or heat.

- Never let anyone smoke around you when handling powder. You'd be courting disaster.

- Always use powder measures when placing powder in your gun. Never pour powder directly from the can, horn, or flask, as there could be a spark remaining in the barrel from a previous shot. This could ignite your entire powder supply.

- Always store powder separately from percussion caps.

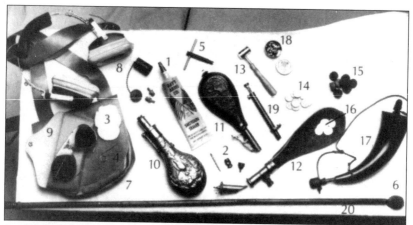

Equipment used in shooting the muzzle-loading shotgun; 1) Wad lubricant 2) Wad puller 3) Cleaning patches 4) Vent pick 5) Nipple wrench 6) Shotgun mop 7) Hunting pouch 8) Ear protection 10) Powder flask 11) Shot flask 12) Shot pouch 13) Shot measure 14) Wads (over powder) 15) Wads (felt) 16) Wads (over shot) 17) Powder horn 18) Percussion caps 19) Powder measure 20) Cleaning rod

Loading Your Muzzle-loading Shotgun

Loading may seem a complicated and time-consuming process. Remember that what you're doing is repeating a process that our ancestors had to go through constantly. With repeated practice, the complexities will become less and less a problem.

Loading will require several accessories:

• Powder flask or horn. This is the receptacle for carrying powder in the field.

• Powder measure. This small container is used to determine the proper amount of powder to use for each shot and to pour it into the muzzle of the shotgun.

• Wads. These fiber spacers are used to form a seal between the powder and shot in the barrel and to retain the load position in the barrel.

• Wad lubricant. This substance is used to lubricate the wads, therefore assuring more effective sealing and some softening of residues that naturally accumulate in the barrel when the gun is fired.

- Wad puller. This instrument is used to remove wads from the barrel in cases where some malfunction prevents the shot from being fired.

- Ramrod with cleaning jag. A standard feature on most muzzle-loading firearms, the ramrod is used to push the charge into the barrel. When used with a cleaning jag, it is also useful in cleaning the inside of the barrel.

- Cleaning patches. Pieces of soft fabric are used to wipe the bore and other hard-to-reach portions of the gun.

- Vent pick. This is a thin wire used to clean the flash channel.

- Nipple wrench. This small wrench is used to remove the nipple of muzzle-loading percussion shotguns.

- Shotgun mop. This is a handy tool for cleaning and lubricating the bore.

- Shooting box or hunting pouch. This is a container for holding all of these items, in addition to your shot, priming powder container (if using a flintlock), and other gear you might find useful.

Before you begin to absorb the loading directions, a few cautions:

- Always wear eye protection when loading or firing your gun. Better be safe than sorry.

- Always wear ear protectors when any firing is done.

- Always follow the loading procedures in the exact order you read them here!

Position the Shotgun for Loading

If you're loading a double-barrel shotgun, you must be very cautious at the beginning. In the case of a percussion gun, if one barrel is still loaded,

Before loading, be sure your shotgun hammer is in the halt cock position and the nipples uncapped.

Place the shotgun between the legs for loading. This is a common and stable position.

make sure its nipple is uncapped and the hammer is at half-cock position. If it's a flintlock, be sure the priming pan is empty, the frizzen open, and the hammer down. Also be careful that you load the empty barrel! It's easy to make a mistake and double the load in one barrel if you're not paying close attention.

Once you've taken these precautions, stand the gun on the ground with the firearm resting between your legs and the muzzle pointed upward and away from you. Never work directly over the muzzle of a shotgun, even when you're sure the gun is unloaded.

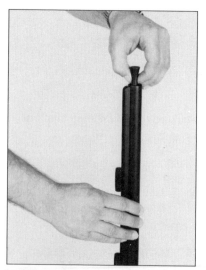

Insert the ramrod to check the bore for a charge (above). At right, remove the ramrod and position the barrel for loading. The bottom part of the ramrod should come to the nipple.

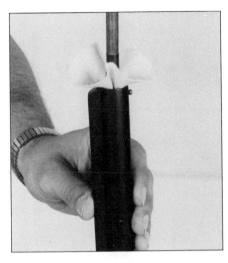

Use a cloth patch to remove any dirt and residue from the bore.

Check Bore for Load

There's an easy way to check this. When your gun is empty, take the ramrod from the stock and insert it as far as it will go into the barrel. Mark a spot on the ramrod flush with the muzzle. Now, to check whether there's a load in the shotgun, put the ramrod down the barrel. If the mark you made when the gun was empty is not at the muzzle, the gun is loaded. If the mark is flush with the muzzle, the barrel is empty. Never try to clear the barrel by yourself. Enlist the aid of an experienced shooter, or, better still, a qualified gunsmith. Never try to free the gun of an old load by firing. You don't know how long the load has been sitting there, what it consists of, or what will happen when you try to fire.

Wipe and Clean the Bore

Before putting in a new charge, remove any lubricant from the inside of the muzzle using a dry shotgun mop. This is also the time to check to see that the ignition channel leading into the barrel is clear. On a flintlock, you can run a pipe cleaner through the flash hole. Also, clean around the pan and frizzen with a brush or cloth to remove oil, dirt, and lint. On a percussion gun, you can clear the channel by firing a few percussion caps with the barrel unloaded. Snapping two or three caps will force any residue or dirt out of the channel and dry the interior as well. To make sure that the barrel is clear, point the muzzle at a blade of grass or other light object when firing the last cap. If the blade moves, it means air is flowing freely through the channel and you're ready for loading.

Always use a powder measure (left) in the loading process. Never load a gun directly from the powder flask.

Measure the Powder Charge

Fill the powder measure to the correct level, taking powder from your horn or flask. Powder charge recommendations are always provided by the manufacturer. Follow them!

The weight of the powder charge is expressed in grains. Each grain equals 1/7,000 of a pound. Powder loads in shotguns are traditionally expressed in drams. A dram is equal to 27.3 grains in weight. The granulation of powder in most main charges in a shotgun is FFg. FFFg is used only in the small-bore guns (20 gauge and under). FFFFg is never used as the main charge. It will burn rapidly and could create dangerous pressure levels. It is used only as a priming agent for flintlocks. The following are the most used loads:

10 gauge	light load	3¼ drams (89 gr.)	1¼ oz. shot
	medium load	3½ drams (96 gr.)	1½ oz. shot
	heavy load	4 drams (109 gr.)	1¾ oz. shot
12 gauge	light load	2¼ drams (76 gr.)	1⅛ oz. shot
	medium load	3 drams (82 gr.)	1¼ oz. shot
	heavy load	3¼ drams (89 gr.)	1¼ oz. shot
16 gauge	light load	2¼ drams (61 gr.)	1 oz. shot
	medium load	2½ drams (69 gr.)	1 oz. shot
	heavy load	2¾ drams (76 gr.)	1⅛ oz. shot
20 gauge	light load	2 drams (55 gr.)	¾ oz. shot
	medium load	2¼ drams (61 gr.)	⅞ oz. shot
	heavy load	2½ drams (69 gr.)	⅞ oz. shot
28 gauge	light load	1¾ drams (47 gr.)	¾ oz. shot
	medium load	2 drams (54 gr.)	¾ oz. shot
	heavy load	2¼ drams (61 gr.)	1 oz. shot

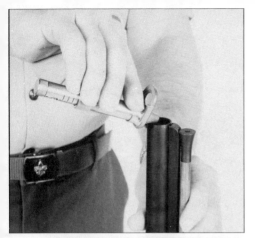

Pour the pre-measured charge directly from the powder measure.

Charge the Barrel with Powder

Being careful to keep the muzzle pointed away from you, pour the powder from your powder measure down the barrel. Tap the side of the barrel a few times with the heel of your hand. This will shake the powder clinging to the sides of the bore all the way down the barrel. If you're using a double-barrel shotgun, develop some kind of system to keep track of which barrel you've loaded first, to prevent "double loading" the same barrel. One way to do this is to temporarily "store" the ramrod in the barrel you are *not* loading while you are loading the other barrel. Remember, never pour powder directly from the powder can, powder horn, or flask.

Load the Wad Column

The next step involves inserting and securing the first two of three wads you will be using in preparing the charge. First place a thin "over powder card wad" (with a thickness of about .125 inch) over the muzzle. Push your ramrod all the way down the barrel so that the wad reaches the powder. The large "button" at the end of the ramrod will straighten the wad as it's rammed into the barrel. When you've rammed far enough to reach the powder charge, apply and maintain a little pressure to compress the wad and the powder together. Holding the wad against the powder for a moment will minimize the chances of air pressure building up between the wad and the powder and creating a gap between the two. If you feel air pressure force the wad and ramrod up, push down again until the air trapped behind the wad bleeds out.

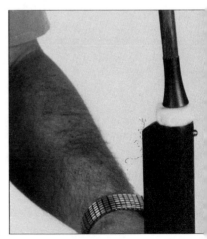

Seat the wad as shown.

Once the wad is firmly seated, follow it with a thick (¼ inch or more) "fiber wad." This second wad may be dampened—but not saturated—with a good black powder lubricant before insertion. Again be sure that this second wad is seated against the first and that both are tight against the powder charge.

Load the Shot

Before inserting the shot, determine what shot is to be used. For trap or skeet shooting, size 7½ to 9 is acceptable. Hunting will require a size ranging from 2 to 8, depending on the game you'll be hunting. The charge can be measured by using a shot dipper or a flask with a built-in measure. Once the proper charge has been measured out, pour it down the bore.

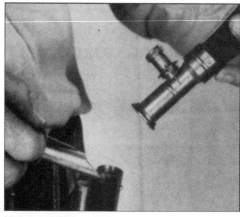

Using a shot measure expedites the loading process.

Load the Over-shot Wad

Finally, take another thin wad and insert it down the barrel as before. Make sure the wad is firmly seated against the shot. Be careful not to apply excessive force as this will deform the soft shot and create an erratic shot pattern when the gun is fired.

After the final wad is firmly seated, again mark the ramrod flush with the muzzle. This will give you a reference to use in future loading so that you will know that the charge and wads are seated correctly each time you load. Note that you have two marks on your ramrod—one to show the depth of the rod when the barrel is empty, and the second to show the depth when loaded.

Once your shotgun is loaded, it's a good idea to mark the ramrod for future reference.

Capping or Priming

The final step before firing is applying the percussion cap, in the case of a percussion gun, or filling the priming pan with a bit of loose powder in the case of a flintlock. This should not be done until you have taken your gun to the actual spot where you intend to fire. In capping or priming, always keep the muzzle pointed downrange or in another safe direction. Once the priming mechanism has been prepared, you are ready to bring the hammer from the half-cock to full-cock position. Pulling the trigger will fire the shot unless there is a misfire.

The final step before firing is cappng the nipple.

Failure to Fire

You pull the trigger, and nothing happens. The main charge doesn't fire. Don't give up. There are a few relatively easy troubleshooting steps you can run through quickly that could solve your problem.

The first thing to remember when you have a misfire is to keep the gun at your shoulder for a couple of minutes, pointed safely downrange. On rare occasions, muzzle-loading shotguns have a delay between the time the trigger is pulled and the time the gun goes off. This is known as "hang fire." It is caused by a slow-to-ignite powder charge.

After waiting that couple of minutes, unshoulder your gun and take a pipe cleaner or fine wire out of your shooting bag. Run this through the nipple or flash hole (on a flintlock) to be sure the channel is open. Recap, or in the case of a flintlock reprime, and try again.

If the gun still won't fire, the problem could be that no powder rests behind the shot. You may have forgotten it during the loading sequence. If you're using a percussion gun, remove the nipple with your nipple wrench. On a flintlock, you can sometimes work sufficient powder behind the charge through the firehole. Cap or prime and try to fire again.

Still no luck? After a reasonable number of corrective efforts, your best course of action is to pull the charge. For this you'll need a strong, sturdy tool. Your standard ramrod may be too delicate or too short to do the job easily. You'll need a stronger, more durable tool, called the work rod. It's best if this rod has a handle to provide additional leverage. The work rod can also be useful in cleaning and loading.

After making sure that your gun is uncapped or unprimed, screw a wad puller onto the end of your work rod. This tool is designed to screw into the wad and give a turning motion. Insert your work rod down the bore and gently screw the wad puller into the top over-shot wad. Bring out the rod and dispose of the wad. Now pour out the shot and retrieve the two remaining wads with the wad puller, one wad at a time. Pour out any powder in the barrel. Thoroughly clean the barrel and flash channel, or nipple, before reloading.

The wad puller is also useful in retrieving cleaning patches that may have fallen off the cleaning jag. Only a foolish shooter would try to remove cleaning patches by shooting them out with powder. Expelling patches this way could cause smoldering fragments of the fabric to remain inside the barrel. They could prematurely ignite the powder the next time you load.

With a flintlock, failure to fire could be caused by a dull piece of flint. Your best bet is to replace the flint with a new piece.

Fouling

Every time you take a shot with a muzzle-loading shotgun, a carbonlike residue is produced and remains in the barrel. This substance is known as fouling. Unchecked, this fouling will collect in the barrel with each shot. After awhile, the gun will become hard to load.

To guard against this, it is recommended that you wipe out the bore of your shotgun after each shot. Simply dampen a cleaning patch that securely fits your muzzle and wipe the entire length of the bore. Run the swab, or patch, through the barrel several times to ensure that all dirt is removed. Follow up with a clean, dry mop or patch. Now you're ready to reload.

Taking Care of Your Gun

A lot of the information in the chapter titled "Shotgun Safety" applies to the care of your muzzle-loader. However, there are a few differences, and you should note them.

You can protect your shotgun by following a basic rule: *Never leave your gun overnight without a thorough cleaning after shooting.* Generally, a simple solution of water and any conventional dishwashing soap, and a bottle of cleaning solvent are all you'll need to keep your gun free of harmful agents. The gun must also be oiled to protect its moving and stationary metal parts. Commercial black powder solvents are effective in removing residue.

Cleaning the Barrel

1. Flushing. With a hooked-breech design, bring the hammer(s) to full cock, remove the ramrod and barrel key(s), and slip the barrel(s) from the stock. Using a mop or patch on your ramrod, saturate the bore and fouling with black powder solvent or with soap and water. Then insert the breech end of the barrel(s) in a bucket of hot, soapy water. With a cleaning rod and attached mop of proper size, "pump" the water up through the bore, moving up and down the full length of the bore several times. Repeat this procedure using clear, hot water and "pumping" until the barrel is clean.

In cases where the breech, barrel, and tang are a single part, it's not a good idea to try to separate the barrel(s). With a percussion gun, you can "siphon" soapy water from a bucket with the use of a flush-out nipple. Remove the standard shooting nipple from your gun with the nipple wrench.

Replace it with a flush-out nipple, which is designed to fit securely in the nipple channel but has a large hole. It can function as the entry point for water. Get a piece of plastic or rubber tubing (the kind used as the fuel line in model airplanes works well) about 18 inches in length. This tubing must be of a diameter to fit securely over the flush-out nipple. Now weight the free end of the tube and place this end in your water bucket. Position the gun so water will flow freely throughout the bore. Use the pumping process described above to scrub and rinse thoroughly. While you're at it, don't overlook your standard shooting nipple. Scrub this piece in the same solution using an old toothbrush and pipecleaner or similar instrument.

A flush-out nipple cannot be used with a flintlock shotgun. With a flintlock, you may use a pipe cleaner to clear out the flashhole, the channel, and the lower end of the barrel. A commercial black powder solvent may be used to cleanse the bore. But be careful! Some of these substances can damage the finish of your stock. Use caution as to

If the barrels can't be removed, use a flush-out nipple and hose.

where you apply them. Scrub up and down the bore with several patches well saturated in a commercial cleaner or soap and water. This may be followed by pouring water in the muzzle and pouring it back out by inverting the barrel to flush out the worst of the fouling. Then wipe the bore again to be sure all the fouling has been removed. If it hasn't, repeat the saturation and flushing process.

2. Drying. Once the barrel has been thoroughly flushed or cleaned, dry the whole apparatus. You can use a dry wool shotgun mop or a series of cloth strips attached to your cleaning rod by a slotted cleaning tip. Pass this fabric through the length of the bore several times. This will dry the metallic surfaces and remove any remaining foreign particles. The job is finished when the fabric comes out both clean and dry.

Cleaning the Lock

Locks are usually attached to the stock with one or two bolts. You'll have to remove the lock(s) for cleaning.

First, set the hammer at half cock. Start unfastening the bolts by unscrewing a few turns. Tap the bolt heads lightly. This will loosen the lock plates from their mortise (their foundation on the stock). You may then proceed with unscrewing the bolts. Once they are removed, carefully lift the lock components off the stock. This can usually be done with simple finger pressure. If you run into trouble, insert a small diameter drift pin from the right-hand lock and tap lightly. This should loosen the left-hand lock to ease its removal. The right-hand lock should now come off easily.

An old toothbrush steamed with very hot water should be fine for removing any fouling and dirt from both sides of the lock. Be sure you cover both sides of the lock. Don't be afraid of hot water. The hotter the water, the faster the lock will dry. Thoroughly wipe dry the entire lock surface. Coat lightly with gun oil and replace.

Finishing Up

Before the gun is reassembled, protect your stock surface by wiping thoroughly with a clean patch or cloth dampened either with water or stock cleaner. Dry thoroughly and follow up with a light application of stock oil or wax preservative.

Before putting all the parts back together, make sure that no moisture from cleaning fluids remains in any of the spaces between the barrel and the stock. If hidden portions are still damp when the gun is assembled, you run a high risk of getting rust in those sensitive places.

Using rubber washers, like those at right, will aid in protecting the shotgun's nipple during dry-firing.

Once your gun is cleaned and oiled, it's ready for storage. Remember to keep it in a cool, dry place. Humidity can cause rusting. The location of your storage area is a matter of personal choice, but many shooters prefer to keep their guns in a locked cabinet or similar secure place.

Learning to Shoot

The material earlier in this pamphlet covers the methods of safety, firing the shot, and shooting at targets.

When dry-firing a muzzle-loader, a little advance preparation is required. The repeated striking of the hammer on the nipple when no cap is covering it calls for protection.

In a percussion gun, the nipple(s) can be protected by fitting with a neoprene or rubber washer such as the one found on a water faucet. Put the washer over the nipple. This will cushion the blow of the hammer and absorb most of the force. If you find the hammer still strikes the nipple, add another washer.

In a flintlock, you can provide similar protection by replacing the flint with a similarly shaped piece of hardwood. This way, you can experience the fall of the hammer and the action of the frizzen without producing wear or tear on either.

Acknowledgements

The Boy Scouts of America is grateful to the National Rifle Association for its assistance in developing the revised requirements for the Shotgun Shooting merit badge. Much of the material used in this new edition of the *Shotgun Shooting* merit badge pamphlet is adapted from the NRA publications *The Basics of Shotgun Shooting* and *The Muzzleloading Shotgun Handbook* and is used with permission.

Boy Scout Standards

Boy Scouts are permitted to fire .22-caliber bolt-action, single-shot rifles, air rifles, shotguns, and muzzleloading long guns under the direction of a certified instructor, 21 years of age or older, within the standards outlined in current Scouting literature and bulletins. BSA policy does not permit the use of handguns in Boy Scouting.

Shotguns

The following standards are established for shotguns to be used by Boy Scouts, Varsity Scouts, or Explorers:

1. It is recommended that either 20-, 16-, or 12-gauge semiautomatic shotguns be used. Gas-operated shotguns are recommended.

2. Ammunition containing No. 8 shot or smaller is recommended on ranges with protected down range of 600 feet. Additional down range distance of 150 feet (total 750) is required for No. 6 shot size. Shot larger than No. 6 is not to be used.

3. Shooting safety glasses and ear protectors are required on shotgun ranges.

4. All training and shooting activities must be supervised by a currently certified NRA shotgun instructor or coach who is 21 years of age or older.

Muzzle Loaders

The following standards pertain to use of muzzleloading long guns by members of the BSA:

1. Muzzleloading rifles must be recently manufactured, percussion only. Recommend .45 or .50 caliber. Rifles made from kits must be checked by an expert gunsmith.

2. Recommended loads of .FFFg blackpowder are not to exceed 1 grain per caliber. One half of this amount is frequently sufficient for target shooting.

3. Shooting safety glasses and ear protectors are required.

4. All training and shooting activities must be supervised by a currently certified NRA and NMLRA muzzleloading rifle instructor over 21 years of age.

5. Each pupil must have one instructor or adult coach under instructor supervision when loading or firing.